D1373093

THE
PRIMARY SOURCE LIBRARY
OF
FAMOUS ARTISTS™

LEONARDO DA VINCI

Catherine Nichols

The Rosen Publishing Group's
PowerKids Press™
PRIMARY SOURCE

New York

For Molly, who's interested in everything

Published in 2006 by The Rosen Publishing Group, Inc.
29 East 21st Street, New York, NY 10010

First Edition

Editor: Kathy Kuhtz Campbell
Book Design: Emily Muschinske
Photo Researcher: Sherri Liberman

Photo Credits: Cover (left) © Erich Lessing/Art Resource, NY, (right), p. 4 (right) © Alinari/Art Resource, NY; p. 4 (left) © Alinari Archives/Corbis; p. 6 (left), courtesy of University of Texas at Austin, Perry-Castañeda Library Map Collection, (right) © David Lees/Corbis; p. 8 (left) © Archivo Iconografico, S.A./Corbis, (right) © Arte & Immagini srl/Corbis; p. 10 © Bridgeman Art Library/Alinari; p. 12 © Ted Spiegel/Corbis, p. 14 (top left) Gabinetto dei Disegni e Stampe, Uffizi, Florence, Italy/Bridgeman Art Library, (bottom left) © Alinari Archives/Corbis, (bottom right) Galleria dell' Accademia, Venice, Italy/Bridgeman Art Library; p. 16 (top) British Museum, London, UK/Bridgeman Art Library, (bottom) © James L. Amos/Corbis; p. 18 AP Photo/Dale Atkins; p. 19 © Alinari Archives/Corbis; p. 20 (top) Bridgeman Art Library/Alinari, (bottom) © Ted Spiegel/Corbis; p. 22 (top) © Ted Spiegel/Corbis, (bottom) © Scala/Art Resource, NY; p. 24 © Erich Lessing/Art Resource, NY; p. 26 (top left and right) © Alinari Archives/Corbis, (bottom) © Réunion des Musées Nationaux/Art Resource, NY; p. 28 © Jan Butchofsky-Houser/Corbis.

Library of Congress Cataloging-in-Publication Data

Nichols, Catherine.
Leonardo da Vinci / Catherine Nichols.— 1st ed.
  p. cm. — (The primary source library of famous artists)
Summary: Introduces Leonardo da Vinci, one of the best-known artists and thinkers of the Renaissance, who was one of the first artists in Italy to experiment with oil paint and whose sketches include designs for a robot, a bicycle, and a helicopter.
Includes bibliographical references and index.
ISBN 1-4042-2762-8 (library binding)
1. Leonardo, da Vinci, 1452–1519—Juvenile literature. 2. Artists—Italy—Biography—Juvenile literature. [1. Leonardo, da Vinci, 1452–1519. 2. Artists. 3. Scientists.] I. Title. II. Series.

N6923.L33N53 2005
709'.2—dc22

                           2003015740

Contents

1	Renaissance Man	5
2	A Tuscan Childhood	7
3	Learning to Be an Artist	9
4	Leonardo's Angel	11
5	Unfinished Business	13
6	The Notebooks	15
7	Looking for a Job	17
8	The Great Horse	19
9	*The Last Supper*	21
10	On the Move	23
11	The Mysterious *Mona Lisa*	25
12	Studies in Science and the Last Painting	27
13	A House in France	29
	Timeline	30
	Glossary	31
	Index	32
	Primary Sources	32
	Web Sites	32

Above: Many people believe that this is Leonardo's self-portrait, or a picture that he drew of himself. He is thought to have drawn it around 1512.

Left: Leonardo drew these flowers sometime between 1480 and 1510. He believed that observing nature carefully was the best way to learn about it.

Renaissance Man

Leonardo da Vinci was one of the most important artists and thinkers of the Italian **Renaissance**. "Renaissance" comes from the French word that means "rebirth." It was a period that started in Italy in the early fourteenth century. During the Renaissance, people studied the ideas and art of ancient Greece and Rome. They also studied the world they saw around them.

Leonardo was curious about art, science, and math. He was interested in the human body and how it worked. During his lifetime, from 1452 to 1519, Leonardo was a painter, a **sculptor**, a **musician**, an inventor, and an **architect**. He became a master of many subjects as did many people of his time. Today people use the words "Renaissance man" or "Renaissance woman" to mean a person who seems to master everything and has great knowledge. Leonardo was one of the first true Renaissance men.

The Milanese under the Visconti, 1339-1402.

- Dominions of Azzo Visconti (1329-1339)
- Acquired by Luchino and Giovanni Visconti (1339-54)
- Bernabò and Galeazzo Visconti (1354-85)
- Gian Galeazzo Visconti (1385-1402)

Areas given a border coloring are those which became dowries for Visconti heiresses, or were otherwise lost, before 1402.

Scale 1:5000000

The Republic of Florence, 1300-1494.

- - - - Boundaries of the Tuscan States in 1300
The Republic of Florence:
- In 1300
- Acquired, 1300 - 1377
- " , 1377 - 1435
- " , 1435 - 1494
- Protected States

Scale 1:5000000

ITALY about 1494.
B.= Bishopric, D.= Duchy,
M.= Marquisate, R.= Republic.

Scale 1:6000000

Above: *Leonardo da Vinci grew up in this stone house in the village of Vinci. "Da Vinci" means "from Vinci."*

Left: *During the fifteenth century, Italy was not one whole country. Instead it was made up of independent city-states and kingdoms. These states and kingdoms were ruled by powerful families who often fought one another.*

A Tuscan Childhood

Leonardo da Vinci was born on April 15, 1452, near the village of Vinci in Italy. Vinci is located in a hilly area called Tuscany. Leonardo's father, Ser Piero, worked as a **notary**. Ser Piero was a rich and well-known person. Leonardo's mother, Caterina, was not. She was a farmer's daughter. Because of this difference, Leonardo's parents were not allowed to marry.

At first Leonardo lived with his mother. Soon after Leonardo was born, his father married a wealthy woman. Ser Piero and his wife did not have children of their own. Perhaps this is the reason Leonardo went to stay with his father and stepmother when he was about two years old.

Ser Piero's work often took him and his wife to the nearby city of Florence. At age five Leonardo was left in Vinci with his grandparents and his uncle Francesco. He walked with his uncle in the family's fields. Francesco taught him about the plants and animals that they saw.

Right: Artist Andrea del Verrocchio made this drawing titled Head of an Angel around 1475. Leonardo studied drawing, painting, and sculpting with Verrocchio from about 1467 to about 1481.

Left: Leonardo made this oil painting of a woman around 1508. He painted this picture about 30 years after he left Verrocchio's workshop. Certain features of the face, such as the eyes, lips, and chin, look like those on Verrocchio's Head of an Angel.

Learning to Be an Artist

As a boy Leonardo drew pictures of the animals and the countryside near his home. Ser Piero noticed his son's skill. He showed some of Leonardo's drawings to Andrea del Verrocchio, a leading artist in Florence. Verrocchio believed that Leonardo had talent. He invited Leonardo, who was about 15 years old, to be an apprentice in his workshop. An apprentice, or assistant, learns a trade by working for an experienced person.

As an apprentice to Verrocchio, Leonardo learned many skills. He learned how to grind, or crush, powders for paints and to mix colors. He prepared wood panels, or the flat surfaces that were used for paintings, by covering them with gesso, a kind of **plaster**. He practiced drawing, painting, and sculpting under the guidance of his teacher, Verrocchio.

Art Smarts

Verrocchio's apprentices worked on paintings at easels, or stands that hold paintings. They helped paint pictures of rich people. They also heated sculptures in hot ovens. Besides doing his work, Verrocchio made sure his assistants did their set tasks. He painted the major parts of a picture and left the simple parts for them to do.

Verrocchio painted Baptism of Christ around 1475. Leonardo painted some of the plants and mountains in this picture. He also painted the angel at the far left. Some people believe that Leonardo had already become more skillful at painting than his teacher.

Leonardo's Angel

In 1472, Leonardo became a member of the Company of Saint Luke's, the painters' **guild** of Florence. As a member Leonardo could get work as an artist. Although he was no longer an apprentice, Leonardo studied in Verrocchio's workshop for about four more years. When he was in his early twenties, Leonardo helped paint Verrocchio's *Baptism of Christ*. The painting shows John the Baptist baptizing Jesus while two angels kneel beside them. Leonardo's job was to paint one of the angels and some of the mountains and plants. Leonardo's angel looks full of life. Many people believe that the other figures in the painting look stiff compared to Leonardo's graceful angel.

Art Smarts

Most artists in Italy in the 1470s used a paint called tempera. In tempera, the ground powder that gives a paint its color is mixed with egg yolk and water. Tempera dries quickly. Leonardo was one of the first Italian artists to paint with oil paint. Oil paint uses linseed oil as a base. Oil paint dries slowly, so an artist can build layers of color.

In Saint Jerome Praying in the Wilderness, Leonardo shows the saint with a lion. One story handed down from earlier times tells of Saint Jerome removing a thorn from a lion's paw. After that, the lion became his companion. Leonardo's lion looks almost lifelike, as does the figure of Saint Jerome.

Unfinished Business

In the early 1480s, after Leonardo had begun to work independently from Verrocchio, he started to paint *Saint Jerome Praying in the Wilderness*. Unfortunately he never completed it. For many years the painting was lost. In 1820, it was found, in two places! The top of the painting was found in a small shop. It had been made into a cupboard door. The rest of the painting was in a shoemaker's shop, where it had been used as the top of a bench. After the painting was repaired, it was hung in a museum in Rome.

During his life Leonardo left many paintings unfinished. One explanation often given for this is that he wanted his paintings to be perfect. If they could not be, he stopped working on them. Another explanation is that once he started a new project, he lost interest in the old one.

Top Left: *Leonardo drew pictures from his imagination, such as this one of a fight between a dragon and a lion.*

Bottom Right: *Leonardo made these funny drawings, which are called caricatures.*

Bottom Left: *This page may be from one of Leonardo's notebooks. It is a drawing of flowers and plans for some of his inventions. He wrote his notes backward, as the close-up (above) shows.*

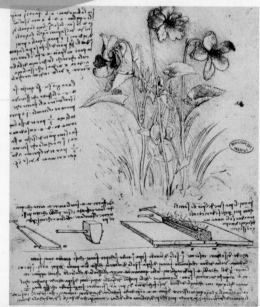

The Notebooks

Leonardo often jotted down his ideas and made sketches, or quick drawings, in notebooks. He drew pictures of unusual-looking people whom he saw on the street. He kept lists of books he owned. He drew plans for buildings. Once he wrote that he had eaten fruit, bean soup, and a salad for lunch. Leonardo wrote that he planned to have his writings printed, but he never did.

Plans for inventions pack the notebooks' pages. Although this was only the late 1400s, he drew plans for a robot, a bicycle, a helicopter, and a parachute. Not all his ideas worked. One idea was put into action in his time, and it is used today. He invented special gates for a waterway. These gates raised or lowered the water level so that boats could travel up or down the waterway.

Art Smarts

All Leonardo's handwriting in his notebooks was penned in a backward type of writing. To read it, a person has to use a mirror. Leonardo was left-handed. Writing from right to left might have kept his sleeves from being smeared with ink. It also might have been easier for him to write that way.

Top: *Leonardo made these drawings that include the outer shell of a tank around 1499. When he moved to Milan in 1482, the city was famous for making weapons. Leonardo hoped that the Duke of Milan would ask him to invent weapons and "machines of war" for the duke's army. He was eager to try his inventions.*

Bottom: *Ludovico Sforza, the Duke of Milan, lived in this castle, which is called the Castello Sforzesco. The duke asked Leonardo to be in charge of all the events and feasts held at the castle.*

Looking for a Job

Besides making artwork, Leonardo sang and played several musical instruments, including the **lyre** and the *lira da braccio*. It is said that he was a handsome man. He had long hair that flowed around his face like a lion's mane. He charmed his friends by telling them funny stories. Although Leonardo had many friends, he also liked to be alone. "If you are alone," he wrote, "you belong entirely to yourself." Leonardo never married.

In 1482, Leonardo decided to leave Florence to seek his fortune in Milan. Before he could go there, he needed to be sure that there would be work for him. Leonardo wrote a letter to Ludovico Sforza, the **Duke** of Milan. He told the duke how he could be of use to him, and he listed his skills. He wrote that he knew how to build bridges and how to make "machines of war." The duke must have liked the letter because he invited Leonardo to come to Milan. The duke became Leonardo's first **patron**.

This bronze statue of a horse is 24 feet (7.3 m) tall and weighs 15 tons (13.6 t). Called Leonardo da Vinci's Horse, it is located in Grand Rapids, Michigan. It is named for Leonardo because it was based on Leonardo's drawings for the Francesco Sforza sculpture. Leonardo never made the statue. This statue, unveiled in 1999, is one of two modern statues of Leonardo's design built in the world. The other is in Italy.

The Great Horse

The Duke of Milan had an important job for Leonardo. He wanted a metal sculpture made of his father, Francesco Sforza, on horseback. Leonardo studied horses and made many sketches of them. He decided to make the statue four times the size of a real horse. It was to be the largest statue ever made. In 1493, the people of Milan got to see a full-size clay model of the statue. Although the model received much praise from the people when Leonardo unveiled it, the statue was never made. The duke needed the metal to make cannons to help guard Milan against French soldiers. Then, in

1499, French soldiers attacked and took over Milan. They used the model for target practice. Leonardo's great horse was destroyed.

This drawing by Leonardo is thought to be one of many studies he made for the Sforza statue.

Above: *Leonardo painted* The Last Supper *in Santa Maria delle Grazie monastery. Many years after Leonardo finished the painting, the monks cut a doorway through the wall and the painting. By 1624, the painting had almost disappeared. In the 1970s, it was successfully cleaned and repaired. This photo was taken after the 1970s cleaning.*

Right: *Visitors look at* The Last Supper.

The Last Supper

In 1495, Leonardo was asked to paint *The Last Supper* on a wall in the dining room of a **monastery** in Milan. *The Last Supper*, a **fresco**, shows Christ and the apostles, or his followers, sharing a meal. Christ is telling the apostles that one of them will turn against him. Each apostle shows surprise in his own way.

It took three years for Leonardo to paint *The Last Supper*. The monks, the men who lived in the monastery, wanted him to paint faster. When it was almost done, only the figure of Judas, the apostle who had turned against Christ, had to be painted. The head monk told Leonardo to finish the work right away. The artist said, in that case, he would use the head monk's face as a model for Judas. The monk let Leonardo finish the work in peace.

Art Smarts

An artist had to work quickly in fresco painting because the painting was made on wet plaster. Leonardo did not like to hurry, so he came up with his own way of painting. He applied a special mix of water-based paints and oil paints to dry plaster. After *The Last Supper* was finished in 1498, however, it began to flake.

21

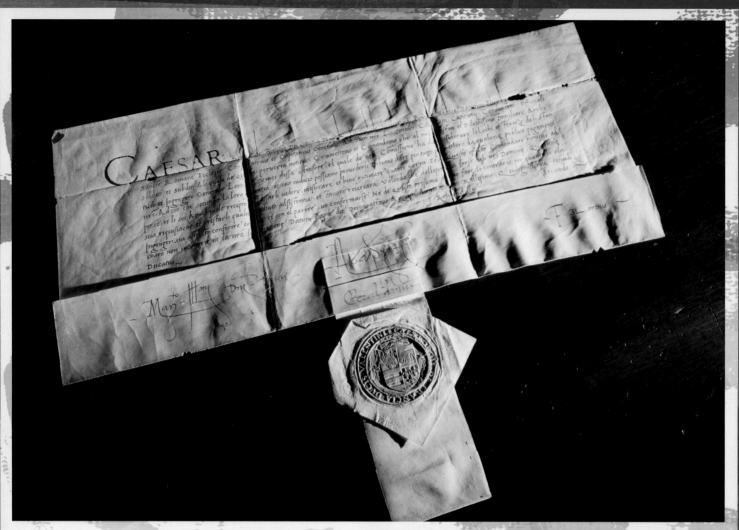

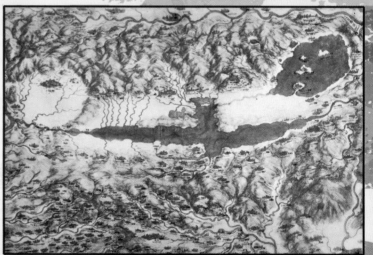

Above: In 1502, Cesare Borgia gave Leonardo this paper, which made Leonardo his senior military architect, or builder, and general engineer.

Right: Leonardo made this map to show some streams and hills in Tuscany. His maps were the most exact ever made at the time, and they helped Borgia's army.

On the Move

Leonardo had a powerful patron in Ludovico Sforza, the Duke of Milan. However, the life he had led in Milan would soon come to an end. In 1499, the French, commanded by King Louis XII, took over Milan. The duke fled the city. Leonardo was left without a patron.

Leonardo spent the next 16 years on the move. In 1500, he went to Mantua, Italy. From there he traveled to Venice and then to Florence. In 1502, he had a new patron and a new job. He became a military **engineer** for Cesare Borgia, a powerful general who was trying to control much of central Italy. As an engineer, Leonardo had many duties. He oversaw the draining of swamps and the digging of waterways. He looked closely at castles to make sure that they were strong. His understanding of measurements helped him to make exact maps, too. After traveling with Borgia's army for about 10 months, Leonardo returned to Florence.

Leonardo painted Mona Lisa, which is also known as La Gioconda, between 1503 and 1506. Most people believe that this painting is the most famous in the world. Leonardo took this painting with him whenever he moved.

The Mysterious *Mona Lisa*

Sometime around 1505, while in Florence, Leonardo painted a woman's portrait. A portrait is a picture of someone. In Europe, the painting is called *La Gioconda*, which in Italian means "the cheerful one." In the United States, however, the painting is called *Mona Lisa*. The woman in the painting is most likely the wife of a businessman, Francesco del Giocondo.

Art Smarts

Leonardo made his subject in *Mona Lisa* seem lifelike by painting dark shadows next to lighter ones. This method is called chiaroscuro. To create a misty effect, he coated the area behind the subject with layers of thin paint to help make shadows hazy. This is called sfumato, which is Italian for "smoky."

There are a few elements in this picture that give it a mysterious quality. One is that the woman's eyes seem to follow the viewer. Another is that she seems to have a hint of a smile. Most people believe that she has a smile because while she was posing, Leonardo hired musicians and jesters to keep her cheerful. The misty background also adds to the painting's mysterious quality.

Top Left: *His early 1480s drawing of two crabs shows how interested Leonardo was in studying nature.*

Top Right: *In his drawing of a dog, Leonardo displays his knowledge of how a dog's body is put together.*

Bottom: *Leonardo painted his last work, Saint John the Baptist, between 1513 and 1516.*

Studies in Science and the Last Painting

After he completed his picture *Mona Lisa*, Leonardo painted fewer paintings. He became more interested in science. To learn how the body worked, Leonardo visited hospitals and watched doctors operate. At the hospital he cut apart the bodies of people who had died. Then he drew what he saw. At his home he also cut up birds, horses, monkeys, and other animals that had already died. He compared the bodies of these animals to those of people.

Leonardo's final painting was *Saint John the Baptist*. Like the woman in *Mona Lisa*, John the Baptist wears a mysterious smile. Most artists of the time painted him as a spirited preacher. Leonardo saw him differently. He made John the Baptist look gentle.

As Leonardo grew older, his health began to fail. Sometime in his sixties he had a stroke and could not use his right arm. He grew tired of moving from one place to another and wanted to find a home.

This was Leonardo's bedroom when he lived at Cloux in Amboise, France. King Francis I of France enjoyed talking with Leonardo and listening to his ideas. Although Leonardo could not paint any longer, he helped plan the king's new castle and a network of waterways. He also took charge of court balls and other events.

A House in France

In his sixties, Leonardo found a place where he could enjoy his last years in comfort. Francis I, king of France, became Leonardo's final patron. He set Leonardo up in a house named Cloux near the king's château, or castle, in Amboise, France. Today the home Leonardo lived in is called Le Clos Luce. The king visited him often. He liked to hear Leonardo talk about his ideas. Francis thought Leonardo was not only a great painter, but also a very wise man.

On May 2, 1519, Leonardo da Vinci died. He was 67 years old. A popular story says that he died while Francis I was visiting him.

Leonardo was a great man. Although many of his paintings have not lasted, the ones that have are masterpieces. His notebooks, too, are full of his wisdom. Page after page of his thoughts, sketches, plans, and inventions show us not only a man who was ahead of his time, but also a true Renaissance man.

Timeline

1452	Leonardo is born on April 15, near the town of Vinci, Italy.
About 1457	Leonardo moves into his grandparents' house in Vinci.
About 1467	He moves to Florence to work as an apprentice in Verrocchio's workshop.
About 1472	Leonardo joins the painters' guild, the Company of Saint Luke's.
About 1475	He helps to paint Verrocchio's *Baptism of Christ*.
About 1481	He works on *Saint Jerome Praying in the Wilderness*.
1482	Leonardo moves to Milan and works for Duke Ludovico Sforza.
1493	He shows the people of Milan the clay model for the Great Horse.
1495	Leonardo starts work on *The Last Supper*.
1499	French troops take over Milan, and Leonardo leaves the city.
1500	Leonardo returns to Florence after being away for almost 18 years.
1502	He begins working for Cesare Borgia in Florence.
About 1505	Leonardo paints *Mona Lisa*.
1513	He begins to paint *Saint John the Baptist*.
1516	Leonardo moves to France.
1519	Leonardo dies on May 2.

Glossary

architect (AR-kih-tekt) Someone who creates ideas and plans for a building.

baptism (BAP-tih-zum) A service done when someone accepts the Christian faith, intended to cleanse a person of his or her sins.

duke (DOOK) A nobleman who is next in rank after a prince.

engineer (en-jih-NEER) A master at planning and building engines, machines, roads, bridges, and canals.

fresco (FRES-koh) A painting done on wet plaster. The word "fresco" also is used to describe the method of painting.

guild (GILD) A group of people who do the same kind of work. The group decides the rules of their trade and sets prices.

lira da braccio (LEE-rah DAH BRAH-choh) A musical instrument that was popular in the Renaissance and that is related to the violin. It has a similar shape to a violin, but has seven strings instead of four and a wider neck.

lyre (LYR) A musical instrument with strings that is like a harp.

monastery (MAH-nuh-ster-ee) A house where people who have taken vows of faith live and work.

musician (myoo-ZIH-shun) A person who writes, plays, or sings music.

notary (NOH-teh-ree) A person who checks law papers and records, such as deeds and business contracts, to make sure that they are real before putting an official seal on them.

patron (PAY-trun) A person who helps someone or something through encouragement or giving money.

plaster (PLAS-ter) A mixture of sand, water, and lime that hardens as it dries.

Renaissance (REH-nuh-sons) The period in Europe that began in Italy in the fourteenth century and lasted into the seventeenth century, during which art and learning flourished.

sculptor (SKULP-tur) A person who makes art by shaping or cutting away material such as clay or stone.

Index

A
apprentice, 9

B
Baptism of Christ,
    11
Borgia, Cesare, 23

C
Company of Saint
    Luke's, 11

D
Duke of Milan, 17,
    19, 23. *See
    also* Sforza,
    Ludovico.

E
engineer, 23

F
Florence, Italy, 7, 9,
    17, 23
Francis I, king of
    France, 29

L
La Gioconda, 25.
    *See also
    Mona Lisa.*
Last Supper, The,
    21
lira da braccio, 17
Louis XII, king of
    France, 23

lyre, 17

M
Mantua, Italy, 23
Milan, Italy, 17,
    19, 21, 23
Mona Lisa, 25, 27.
    *See also La
    Gioconda.*

N
notebooks, 15, 29

R
Renaissance, 5, 29

S
*Saint Jerome Praying
    in the
    Wilderness,*
    13
*Saint John the
    Baptist,* 27
Sforza, Francesco,
    19
Sforza, Ludovico,
    17, 23. *See
    also* Duke of
    Milan.

V
Verrocchio, Andrea
    del, 9, 11
Vinci, Italy, 7

Primary Sources

Cover. Left. *Lady with an Ermine.* Leonardo. Around 1490. Oil on walnut. Czartorysky Museum. Cracow, Poland. **Right and Page 4, Right.** *Self-Portrait.* Thought to be by Leonardo. Drawing. Biblioteca Reale. Turin, Italy. **Title Page.** *Drawing of Four Horse Legs.* Leonardo. Created sometime between 1470 and 1518. **Page 4. Left.** *Pencil Drawing of Flowers.* Leonardo. Drawn sometime between 1480 and 1510. **Page 6. Top.** "Leonardo da Vinci's house." Leonardo's childhood home in the village Vinci, in the region of Tuscany, Italy. **Page 8. Right.** *Head of an Angel.* Andrea del Verrocchio drawing, charcoal and brush, around 1475. The Uffizi Gallery. Florence. **Left.** *Female Head (La Scapigliata).* Leonardo. Oil on panel. Around 1508. It is thought to be an unfinished painting of the Madonna. Galleria Nazionale. Parma. **Page 10.** *Baptism of Christ.* Andrea del Verrocchio and Leonardo. Around 1475. Oil on panel. Uffizi Gallery. Florence. **Page 12.** *Saint Jerome Praying in the Wilderness.* Leonardo. This unfinished painting was worked on around 1480. The Vatican Museums and Galleries. Vatican City, Rome. **Page 14. Top.** *Fight Between a Dragon and a Lion.* Leonardo's drawing in brown ink with wash on paper. Gabinetto dei Disegni e Stampe. Uffizi, Florence. **Bottom Left.** *Drawing of Flowers and Diagrams.* Made sometime between 1490 and 1519. Possibly from one of Leonardo's notebooks. **Bottom Right.** *Seven Studies of Grotesque Faces.* Attributed to Leonardo. Red chalk on paper. Done from about 1495 to the early 1500s. Galleria dell' Accademia. Venice, Italy. **Page 16. Top.** *Drawing of the Shell of Tanks.* Leonardo. The British Museum. London, England. **Bottom.** "Corner Tower at the Sforza Castle." Milan, Italy. The Dukes of Milan lived in this castle. Leonardo completed frescoes in a part of the building called the pergola. **Page 19.** *A Horseman Trampling on a Fallen Foe.* A study for the Sforza statue in Milan done around 1488, with silverpoint on blue paper. From an original in the Royal Collection at Windsor Castle by permission of Her Majesty Queen Elizabeth II. **Page 22.** *The Last Supper.* Painted from 1495 to 1498, in the refectory of Santa Maria delle Grazie. Milan. **Page 22. Top.** Cesare Borgia's Commission for Leonardo to become general, issued around 1502. The Duke of Milan gave Leonardo the rank of general and made him senior military architect and general engineer for inspecting Rome and building fortifications. **Bottom.** Map of Arezzo and the Val di Chiana. Leonardo's map drawn around 1495. Facsimile of the original in the Windsor Collection. Great Britain. **Page 24.** *Mona Lisa.* Also called *La Gioconda.* Oil on wood, painted between 1503 and 1506. The Louvre. Paris, France. **Page 26. Top Right.** *Drawing of a Dog.* Leonardo. Drawn between 1470 and 1519. **Top Left.** *Drawing of Two Crabs.* Leonardo. Around 1482. **Bottom.** *Saint John the Baptist.* Leonardo's last painting, which he worked on between 1513 and 1516. The Louvre. Paris, France. **Page 28.** "Bedroom of Leonardo da Vinci at the Château du Clos Luce." Amboise, France.

Web Sites

Due to the changing nature of Internet links, PowerKids Press has developed an online list of Web sites related to the subject of this book. This site is updated regularly. Please use this link to access the list: www.powerkidslinks.com/psla/leonardo/